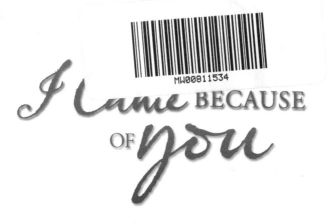

I Came BECAUSE OF you

ADVENT & CHRISTMAS MEDITATIONS

W | warnerpress®

Copyright © 2018 Warner Press, Inc.
Printed in the United States of America
All rights reserved
305800212149

I Came Because of You

I did not come for praise or fame,
For songs or endless cheer;
Leaving Heaven's perfect peace,
I came to draw you near.

I did not come to rule the world
Like warriors and kings.
I came to rescue you from death;
A righteous throne, I bring.

I came not to condemn the world;
I came in love and truth
To reconcile you to My heart:
I came because of you.

*God did not send his Son into the world to condemn
the world, but to save the world through him.*

JOHN 3:17 (NIV)

Great Joy

You are My great joy. If you were the only person who walked this earth, I still would have left heaven's perfection to be with you. I desire to share My glory with you so you know My heart is for you.

I bring you good tidings of great joy.

LUKE 2:10

The Baby Jesus

I took My first breath the same as you.

I cried from hunger the same as you.

I began My life vulnerable and dependent,
the same as you.

I came as a baby, fully human,
and entered your world the same as you

so I could bring you into My world
for all eternity.

This will be a sign to you: You will find a baby
wrapped in cloths and lying in a manger.
LUKE 2:12 (NIV)

Everlasting Father

This is what it means for Me to be your Father:
When you come to Me, broken, I will lift your head.
When you are tired, I will give you rest.
When you need guidance, I provide direction.
When you ask for forgiveness, I offer grace,
and then I throw a party on your behalf.

He will be called…Everlasting Father.
Isaiah 9:6 (NIV)

Seek and Find

The shepherds found Me
 By following a star
  And opening their hearts to My love;
The wise men found Me
 By traveling afar,
  Their eyes on My light from above.
You also can find Me
 Wherever you are,
  Find the joy and peace I impart,
If like the faithful who followed My star,
 You seek Me with all of your heart.

*You will seek me and find me when you seek me
with all your heart.*

JEREMIAH 29:13 (NIV)

Evil is Defeated

Satan tried everything in his power to keep Me from coming. He knew if I came to earth, his days would be numbered. And because of today's horrific evils, he wants you to believe I am powerless. The truth is, I defeated Satan when I arrived 2,000 years ago, and I can defeat him in your life today. My birth ended the war, and My death and resurrection confirm it.

Resist the devil, and he will flee from you.

James 4:7 (NIV)

Prince of Peace

I am peace. You might experience peace in other things or people, but that kind of peace is momentary. I bring lasting peace. True peace can never be separated from My presence. You can experience eternal peace when you allow Me, the Prince of Peace, to guard your heart and mind.

He will be called…Prince of Peace. Of the greatness of his government and peace there will be no end.

Isaiah 9:6–7 (NIV)

Unexpected Hope

No one expected hope to arrive as a newborn baby. People look to royalty to provide a majestic king. They look to the military to send out powerful troops. They look to the government to promote justice for the oppressed. The last place anyone would look for delivery from hardship is in a stable. Yet I delight in the unexpected. Unlike the world teaches, I tell you the least will be greatest, the last will be first, and the seekers will find. I know your need. Deliverance has come.

The deliverer will come from Zion.

ROMANS 11:26 (NIV)

A State of Mind

Christmas is not a time or season
but a state of mind.

To cherish peace and good will,
to be plenteous in mercy,
is to have the real spirit of Christmas.

If you think on these things,
you will experience this season anew.

All over, around, and within you
will shine My light,
radiating hope to all the world.

Be transformed by the renewing of your mind.
ROMANS 12:2 (NIV)

Emmanuel

I am not a distant God.

I am not an indifferent God.

I am not an unsympathetic God.

I know you, I am for you, and I am with you.

This is the meaning of Emmanuel.

A virgin shall be with child, and shall bring forth a son, and they shall call his name Emmanuel, which being interpreted is, God with us.

MATTHEW 1:23

Generosity

Generosity is the hallmark of the Christmas season. People share their gifts with one another, and they share their financial resources to help those in need. Generosity is also the foundation for the Christmas season. My Father's kindest, most generous act He offered came on the very first Christmas when He gave the world a Savior.

He saved us through the washing of rebirth and renewal by the Holy Spirit, whom he poured out on us generously through Jesus Christ our Savior.

TITUS 3:5–6 (NIV)

The Light

This Christmas, see Me for who I am.

I am light.

I dispel darkness to shine in your heart.

I offer eternal, life-giving sight to your spiritual blindness.

You don't just follow the light, you *have* the light.

You have Me.

I am the light of the world. Whoever follows me will never walk in darkness, but will have the light of life.

JOHN 8:12 (NIV)

Room at the Manger

I made the journey
   from heaven to earth,
fulfilling God's plan
   through My human birth.

With an angel chorus
   and a starlit sky,
shepherds and cattle
   heard My cry.

Soon wise men came
   their gifts to bring
and left their hearts
   as an offering.

And there's room for you
   at the manger still
to celebrate Jesus
   and to know My will.

I am gentle and humble in heart.
MATTHEW 11:29 (NIV)

Messiah

I am not just the Messiah,
I am *your* Messiah.
You need not look for Me,
for when I arrived that
first Christmas morning,
I found you.

We have found the Messiah.
JOHN 1:41 (NIV)

Celebrate My Gifts

My arrival brings many gifts from the Father…

My love that's stronger than your shortcomings,

My grace that's mightier than your mistakes.

My hand that lifts you above your circumstances,

My Word that is more durable than your
    disappointments.

My peace that's steadier than your surroundings,

My presence that's more infinite than the earth.

The gift of God is eternal life in Christ Jesus our Lord.
ROMANS 6:23 (NIV)

God Incarnate

This is the world's greatest blessing:
To reach into the manger,
and touch the hand of God.

He will be called…Mighty God.

Isaiah 9:6 (NIV)

Life in My Name

The angels sang it,
The shepherds claimed it,
The wise men found it…
Life in My name.

When you say it,
If you claim it,
Once you'll believe it, you'll find
Life in My name.

Jesus is the Messiah, the Son of God, and…by believing you may have life in his name.
JOHN 20:31 (NIV)

King of Kings

Earthly kings assert their power;
I gave up My power.

Earthly kings amass great wealth;
My treasures are in heaven.

Earthly kings conquer countries;
I overthrow death.

Earthly kings wield the sword;
I extend grace.

I came as a baby, but I am also your King.

*On his robe and on his thigh he has this name
written:* KING OF KINGS AND LORD OF LORDS.
REVELATION 19:16 (NIV)

Chosen

You are chosen by Almighty God,
Creator of the Universe.
I equip you for life.
I empower you with love.
I anoint you with strength.
I bestow dignity and purpose to you.

*The LORD, who is faithful, the Holy One of Israel...
has chosen you.*
ISAIAH 49:7 (NIV)

Receive the Message Anew

This Christmas, receive My message as if you are hearing it for the first time: I have come to set you free! I have come to redeem the broken world, to make things right, and to bring you joy.

He has sent me to bind up the brokenhearted.

ISAIAH 61:1 (NIV)

Mary's Song

Like My young daughter Mary,
may your heart also sing:

My soul glorifies the Lord
and my spirit rejoices in God my Savior,
for he has been mindful
of the humble state of his servant.

LUKE 1:46–48 (NIV)

Celebrate the Season

Celebrate the season,
carol loud and long.

Join the smiling chorus;
sing the angels' song.

Let your heart be happy;
laugh and love and live.

Know the peace and purpose
only I can give.

Give thanks to God the Father,
for all that Christmas brings.

Celebrate the season;
welcome Me, your King.

*Where is the one who has been born king of the
Jews? We saw his star when it rose and have come
to worship him.*

MATTHEW 2:2 (NIV)

The Greatest Gift

When you receive an amazing gift, you tell others about it. This season, be bold and brave: tell others about the greatest gift of all.

We have seen and testify that the Father has sent his Son to be the Savior of the world.

1 JOHN 4:14 (NIV)

A Time for Gladness

Christmas is a time for gladness, a time for slowing down and enjoying the simple things life offers. In a child's laughter, in a friendly smile, in a gentle touch or hug, you extend My peace and love to the world.

Worship the LORD with gladness; come before him with joyful songs.

PSALM 100:2 (NIV)

Remember the Reason

In the hustle of the season
And the hurry of your way,
Remember I'm the reason
You honor Christmas day.

So sing triumphant carols
And don your tree with lights,
Then celebrate the Christ child
Who brings eternal life.

This is eternal life: that they know you, the only true
God, and Jesus Christ, whom you have sent.
JOHN 17:3 (NIV)

Where Your Treasure Is

Of all the gifts you give and receive this Christmas,
treasure Me the most.

For when you treasure
Me the most,

then you experience the true gift of Christmas.

Where your treasure is,
there your heart will be also.

MATTHEW 6:21 (NIV)

God's Mercy

Mercy and grace come wrapped
In swaddling cloths,
Redemption arrives
In a baby's cries.
The gift of salvation
Is our celebration
Delivered by God
To the heart.

The tender mercy of our God...
will come to us from heaven.
LUKE 1:78 (NIV)

Beckoning Star

Instead of exploding fireworks across the heavens or writing words in the clouds, God called a star, planted it above Israel, and beckoned you gently to Me with a twinkle from the night, whispering, "This is my beloved Son, your Savior."

We saw his star when it rose and have come to worship him.

MATTHEW 2:2 (NIV)

New Joy

When you seek Me and find Me, you find not what you think you want, but what you need. You will find new delights in My fellowship and company. Let Me be your gift.

Your joy will be complete.

Deuteronomy 16:15 (NIV)

Welcome Home

I entered the world as a child, but through God, I am also your Father. Before the foundation of the world was made, I adopted you into My family and made you part of My family tree. Welcome home!

To all who did receive him, to those who believed in his name, he gave the right to become children of God.

JOHN 1:12 (NIV)

Come to the Manger

Come to the manger
Where you will find peace;
Kneel at the manger
Where innocence sleeps.
Behold Me, the Christ child,
Humble and mild,
Then worship your Savior
In the face of this child.

The shepherds returned, glorifying and praising God for all the things they had heard and seen.
LUKE 2:20 (NIV)

The Word

"Logos" is the original Greek word for "The Word." But there is another meaning most people do not talk about. "Logos" also means "the reason for life." I am Logos, The Word, I am the reason for life, and I welcome you into all that My life offers.

The Word became flesh and made his dwelling among us. We have seen his glory.

JOHN 1:14 (NIV)

Linger

Linger in My love. Feel My presence in your heart. Inhale grace and exhale gratitude. Let go of worry, and instead, worship Me and feel My glorious wonder.

Grow in the grace and knowledge of our Lord and Savior Jesus Christ. To him be glory both now and forever!

2 PETER 3:18 (NIV)

The Gift & The Giver

You desire to give gifts to those you love, and you go to great lengths to do so. You give to show the depth of your love to family and friends. Yet I give the gift that will never be outgrown or never go out of style: eternal life.

If you, then, though you are evil, know how to give good gifts to your children, how much more will your Father in heaven give good gifts to those who ask him!

MATTHEW 7:11 (NIV)

Wonderful Counselor

I came to be your counselor. I came to walk alongside you, be present with you. You are safe with Me to share your hurts, fears, anxieties, and concerns. In turn, I will encourage you and share the real truth as opposed to manmade truth. Your Wonderful Counselor is available, approachable, and waiting.

To us a child is born, to us a son is given....
And he will be called Wonderful Counselor.
ISAIAH 9:6 (NIV)

Become a Child

See Christmas this year through the eyes of a child. Rediscover the joy and wonder. Be amazed at the telling of My arrival to earth as a baby. Unleash your unrestrained capacity to love. Abandon your cynicism, embrace the truth of My love, then worship Me in your childlike faith.

Anyone who humbles himself as this little child is the greatest in the Kingdom of Heaven.
MATTHEW 18:4 (TLB)

Fear Not!

When I came to your world, the angels commanded the shepherds, *Do not be afraid* (Luke 2:10, NIV). The same is true today. Whatever you face, hand your fears to Me. Then, like the angels of long ago, celebrate My presence.

God hath not given us the spirit of fear;
but of power, and of love, and of a sound mind.

2 TIMOTHY 1:7

I Choose You

Before the world was formed, I already knew you. Before you took your first breath, I had already said "yes" to you. Before I arrived that first Christmas day, I knew I would come for you. Even before you walked away from Me, I loved you with an everlasting love. You don't have to earn My love. Just receive it in the grace I give it.

Because of his kindness, you have been saved through trusting Christ. And even trusting is not of yourselves; it too is a gift from God.

Ephesians 2:8 (TLB)

Christmas Gifts

The happiness of Christmas
Is so many special things:
The wonder in a child's bright eyes,
The cards the postman brings,
Presents underneath the tree,
The family gathered there,
The red and green of holly boughs,
The spicy scented air,
The Christmas story being read,
The blazing Star above,
And over all the gentle peace
Of My abundant love.

Thanks be to God for his indescribable gift!
2 CORINTHIANS 9:15 (NIV)

Come & Behold

The world is all alight with the holidays. People seem happier. Children seem gladder. Choirs sing louder. And homes seem brighter. Somewhere, deep inside of all of us, we know: the magic is in the Messiah, our rapture in our Redeemer. Come and behold, not just at Christmas, but every day.

The LORD turn his face toward you and give you peace.

NUMBERS 6:26 (NIV)

Why I Came

Believing that I came and believing *why* I came can be two very different things. I am not just a feel-good Christmas story; I *am* the story of redemption. I am not just a good person; I am your Lord. I didn't come just to live on earth; I came to save you. I am Emmanuel, and I came for *you*.

The Lord himself will choose the sign—
a child shall be born to a virgin! And she shall
call him Immanuel (meaning, "God is with us").
Isaiah 7:14 (TLB)

Jesus

Say My name out loud. Let the sounds flow from your heart and rush off your tongue. Become familiar with My name, much as a child is familiar with her parents' names or an individual is with his best friend's name. I long to be your friend and confidant, but even more, I came to be your Savior and Lord. Find My glory in My name.

You are to give him the name Jesus, because he will save his people from their sins.

<small>MATTHEW 1:21 (NIV)</small>

Your Greatest Joy

My child, you are so precious to Me that I will not allow the commercialism of Christmas to become your god. When I become your greatest desire, I also become your greatest joy, and your heart will be full.

Father, I want those you have given me to be with me…and to see my glory.

JOHN 17:24 (NIV)

Spread the Word

I chose the shepherds to share the good news of My arrival to earth. I didn't choose kings, wealthy people, or famous celebrities. I appointed common people with simple hearts and gentle hands who would welcome Me without hesitation and obey the angels without question. Uninhabited by status and eager to share, they *spread the word concerning what had been told them about this child, and all who heard it were amazed* (Luke 2:17–18, NIV). You, too, will find great joy when you spread the Good News of great joy to others.

An Infinitely Divine Happiness

The irony of Christmas is I did not come to earth for Myself. My heart is content with our Father. I came so you can experience the infinitely divine happiness found only in Me.

My glory. My love. My grace.

I came for you. I came because of you.

The world will know you sent me and will understand that you love them as much as you love me. Father, I want them with me...so that they can see my glory.

JOHN 17:23–24 (TLB)

Thanks to the following writers who contributed to this devotional:

p. 7; 41: Virginia Richardson

p. 11: Calvin Coolidge

p. 17: Julie Swihart

p. 24: A. Marie Herrmann

p. 15: Robin K. Fogle

p. 46: Rebecca Barlow Jordan